Sticky is pungent, viscous, alchemical, a laying on of hands. It is a sensorium of beeswax, turpentine, blood, yeast, coconut oil, melted buttercream, Crisco—rubbed into surfaces and crevices of memory, printing presses, diner tabletops, bathroom stalls, births, seductions, lovers. *Sticky* coaxes one and all to ferment, to open every which way, to give over to the exploration and cravings of Carter Steinmann's "dirty fingers" and capable poetics.
—Rebekah Edwards

Sticky is both tart and sweet, feminine and masculine, gentle and rough. Steinmann writes, "Women who turn me on / and simultaneously make my heart hurt / where do you come from / how do you do what you do?" This collection of poems demonstrates the act of loving and desiring women. *Sticky* will leave your heart throbbing and craving more.
—Carina Yun

Carter Steinmann's poetry doesn't shy away from love's messy and dangerous moments—rather, these poems "ask first / then show no mercy." Their dirty, sticky hands explore the body, breathing its "fermenting sourdough," "bergamot and sawdust," then dare "ask for more." Like a fresh wound—sensitive and seeping, tender and exposed—Steinmann's syntax is hot to the touch and raw. These poems understand desire's spellwork, and refuse to doll-up pleasure; rather, with unabashed candor and an unblinking eye, without fear or apology, we see the carnal as it is. These poems ache. They "drive home too drunk." They "fuck a Vandercook." They stick a dirty finger in your mouth. And it is delicious.
—Flower Conroy

Sticky

sticky

Carter Steinmann

Sticky

HEADMISTRESS PRESS

Copyright © 2016 by Carter Steinmann.
All rights reserved.

ISBN-13: 978-0692585931
ISBN-10: 0692585931

This book may not be reproduced, in whole or in part, including illustrations, in any form (beyond that permitted by Sections 107 and 108 of the U.S. Copyright Law and except by reviewers for the public press), without written permission from the publishers.

Cover art © 2014 by Carter Steinmann.
Cover & book design by Mary Meriam.

PUBLISHER
Headmistress Press
60 Shipview Lane
Sequim, WA 98382
Telephone: 917-428-8312
Email: headmistresspress@gmail.com
Website: headmistresspress.blogspot.com

For Jency

Contents

Buttercream	1
Desert Flood	2
A_Mommy	4
Milkthistle	6
Thrush	7
Sticky	8
How Many Women	9
Beeswax and Turpentine	10
Toolbelt	11
Louise and Slutty Cat	12
Printing	13
Acknowledgments	15
About the Author	15

Buttercream

Creamsicle birthday cake
pink yellow blue candles seep
melted in buttercream frosting
dirty finger in my mouth in your mouth
hear me now when I say
I feel some type of way.

Candied clavicle asks for more
where are the curves of my body?
Hidden under grandma's dress
restrained in tight black pants
seams rub, fabric splits
velvet inner thigh spills soft
engorged and plump.
Women who turn me on
and simultaneously make my heart hurt,
where do you come from
how do you do what you do?

Desert Flood

Windows down
beating wind assaults
floods my head
disrupts collected dust on the dashboard
holes fill and
I'm underwater
on the desert highway
boots flood with sand
mouth floods with sand

lookin' out the rearview mirror,
I am Louise—
my time is measured in
payphone calls from gas stations

I imagine Thelma in the seat next to me
applying lipstick, a merlot shade
sticking a painted finger, a crimson shade
in the cigarette lighter

pulled off the highway,
curled up in the backseat of the ford,
I lay among the cans of black beans
and bag of trailmix,

bent knees
balled up flannel under head,
susan sontag lulls me to that place
sandy and surreal

> *After being 'femme' to H and 'butch' to L,*
> *I recall finding greater physical satisfaction*
> *in being 'passive,' though emotionally*
> *I am definitely the lover type, not the beloved…*

I drive until the sky is that color
periwinkle dusk straight ahead,
peach sherbert in the rear view mirror

at a roadside diner
coffee clings fuzzy to my teeth
tastes of copper and charcoal
I'm knitting with butcher's twine
and it's making me soft again—
the waitress calls me darlin'
and I melt
to a puddle on the floor

Note: Lines in italics excerpted from *Reborn: Journals and Notebooks 1947-1963* by Susan Sontag

A_Mommy

say honey
say sugar

fed me warm milk and drew a bath
her running shorts
thighs ripple pucker soft
her cotton t-shirt
breasts droop like this—

Amazing Grace—her one hand
cradled my limp neck
relaxing into complete abandon
[eyes roll back dull]
the other scooped bathwater
onto my soapy hair

"Don't stay in too long, Sugar"

I rise pruned and blotchy
wrapped me up in a towel
rubbed lotion down my legs

put on the shirt I never wash
smells like me—
bergamot and sawdust

milk heating on the stove
coconut oil on the night stand
dick in the harness on the floor

break me in—soft glove
raise something in me

she took me out dancing
leather soles on wood
slow, slow
        quick-quick
hand on my waist, I swooned

mommy is coming—
takes me in her car
takes me home
takes me on the kitchen table

break me in like—
my father's baseball mitt
soft leather glove

after, she'd put me on her lap,
rub my back,
sing me a song

Milkthistle

she swallowed me whole when I was twenty-six. she swallowed all of me

    time lapse

a woman more than six months pregnant stands naked in the sunlight the infant within her experiences a golden haze. the noises of her mothers' body reach her: joints cracking, intestinal rumblings

    time lapse

ephemeral belly bloom now hollow becomes nest
chafe swollen throbbing gentle

    dutch tilt

milkthistle tea brewing in a jar on the counter

    time lapse

iron-rich skin swells tight white, rusted freckles, hip hugger jeans, your mother's wrinkled shirt, in the truck with my sister, blackberries cradled in her lap

Thrush

the body as a site of—
petrichor: the pleasant earthy smell
after a night rain

that night, in our bed,
you smelled like sourdough starter
just this once—

she gave it to me one easter
in a mason jar

she gave it to me that night
with dirty fingers

rise beneath my hands
fermenting sourdough
your loaf blooming
lactobacilli and yeasts
ask for more

Sticky

why you// on the drive back home
like sticky[?]//after one beer too many
sticky like when you// four smokes too many I thought
touch the bark of a tree// about going down on you
and the sap rubs off // on your period
you've punctured its shell// if you came home with me
and oozed it to palm// you told me of the pleasure that morning
never come off// of bleeding on your fingers for the first time
not matter how you scrub// in years that damn IUD been there since 2010
sticky like elmer's glue// driving past the lake
squeezed into the palm of your hand// I imagined you in my bed
sticky like cum//I'll eat your raw bloody snatch
before it dries clear and crusty// til it's medium-rare
to the peach fuzz on your lower back// think myself sick, salmonella
sticky like tape that's never sticky enough// when I got back home
sticky like being on a bus in the rain// I found I was bleeding too
windows fogged up seats slushy// subtle at first will be gushing by morning
bodies muggy beneath wool sweaters// in the VW bus clots dangle sticky
sticky like the inside of a fig// staining my thighs at the
sticky like dried apricots in a plastic bag// gas station carwash bathroom
sticky like handles on kitchen cabinets// birthday girl gets what she wants
sticky like babies' hands// when I turned 21 we went to the ruby room too but
after eating watermelon//everyone was too sober and
sticky like molasses //there were too many bros and
thick and slow//I was on the rag and
sticky like tabletops at roadside diners //my girlfriend didn't go down on me
that get wiped down millions of times //not that I would've let her
but yet still are always sticky //but that's not the point

How Many Women

They made me do it
be your puppy dog
teach you how to spit
take shots in the kitchen
chain smoke almost everyday
pee on the sidewalk
stand in it while making out
they make me do things I'm not proud of.

I can't understand what has taken over
it's the Stella Artois the Negra Modelo
the Lagunitas and cheap red wine
stains and crusts intersection of lip and gum
and the intimacy of sharing a cigarette.

Can't I just use your bathroom
the door in the back
past all these dykes
black leather greased hair
a sea of old spice
place my ass on the toilet
read the shit on the walls
how many women have fucked here?
no cum no evidence
just *Long Live the Lex.*

Beeswax and Turpentine

These hands will knead open
thick rich slob leaves me dry
encourage the tearing
help the healing
thumbing the seed in
these hands will pull muscle and bones from
a ripe, swollen vessel
will bathe in white yellow green gunk,
blood and shit,
catch and release.

These hands will continue to crack
knuckles swelling year by year
nails filled with smut
will ache more
will sand smooth
release wet soon cracked and ashy,
beeswax and turpentine.

These hands will dig deep
knees throb and snap,
fingers slick with coconut oil
wilted back sore and aching
salted upper lip,
will ask first
then show no mercy.

Will churn and knead
and gently beckon
furrowed brow blocks no light,
find the spot
lose it then find it again
these hands will be lost
and will come home.

Toolbelt

Give me a toolbelt thick and heavy,
these hips can open doors
can support a tired crooked arm
can jut out and sink in to women
can rest an infant on one and a toddler on the other
and these hips can hold a 15 lb. toolbelt.

Wifebeater sports bra tightfitted pants
my genderfuck free
I'll fix your leaky faucet lil lady
be your firefighter-carpenter
take you home
sand you smooth
extinguish your lungs.

Gentle swarm body
pile of meat raw red
thaw room temperature
I've always wanted to be a butcher
blue collar, male dominated, romanticized
occupations that turn me on
not like that like this.

Starchy uniform drape my body
loyal worker eroticized
mailman firefighter carpenter
construction worker handyman
plumber truck driver butcher

put my back into it
dirty up my hands
come home
remove socks
eat meatloaf.

Louise and Slutty Cat

louise and slutty cat walk into a bar
bartender keeps shoving
elbows on sticky coated wood
whiskey gingers keep em coming
slutty cat getting cruised by bad cop
louise accidentally flagging anal sex
makeup smudged everywhere
fake blood drips into eyes
louise gives slutty cat cigarettes
slutty cat says louise is masculinefeminine
in the smoking room
up against the pool table
bum more smokes
talk it out act it out try it out
wearing each other's clothes
louise and slutty cat pet all night
black velvet and a shirt that suggests
"we are not just good friends"
louise's blood gets on slutty cats' collarbone
and slutty cats' lil black nose smears onto louise's cheeks
once thelma goes to sleep slutty cat finishes the leftovers
from a plate louise left out
drive home too drunk take the 13
it's faster than 580
BZ music high-beams on
peppermint tea in the kitchen
louise sits slurping on the counter
slutty cat gets loose lets it happen
legs wrap hands creep louise gets wild
whiskers nose black
blood goopy red
bruises blue green
smoosh smear across faces til
louise and slutty cat are marked murky

Printing

Let me bury my waist in the printing press
unlatch the reel rod ratchet
grasp packing and drawsheet
loosen the screws in the gripper bar
face down, bent in half
I'll fall over the feed table
pack me tight.

Scrape cobalt blue ink across my love handles
roll me over text block your sans serif too sharp
proof me on newsprint first then
tuck thick creamy paper into my belly button
and roll us through together.

Trinkets interlock gadgets
brass clicks and clunks
heavy machinery gestures me in,
this is how I fuck a Vandercook.

When you're done grease me up with crisco
soak me every inch with a clean, folded rag
if my hinges are worn
garnish me with vaseline thick and goopy
thoroughly saturated wipe me clean
til my sides shine lanolin soft.

Acknowledgments

Many thanks to Rebekah Edwards, Stephanie Young, and Anna Cornelius.

Thanks to the editors of *Humble Pie Literary Journal* for publishing "Sticky" and "Toolbelt."

About the Author

Carter Steinmann is a poet, sculptor, dancer, woodworker, and doula. She lives in Oakland, CA and received her undergraduate education at Mills College.

Headmistress Press Books

Lovely - Lesléa Newman
Teeth & Teeth - Robin Reagler
How Distant the City - Freesia McKee
Shopgirls - Marissa Higgins
Riddle - Diane Fortney
When She Woke She Was an Open Field - Hilary Brown
God With Us - Amy Lauren
A Crown of Violets - Renée Vivien tr. Samantha Pious
Fireworks in the Graveyard - Joy Ladin
Social Dance - Carolyn Boll
The Force of Gratitude - Janice Gould
Spine - Sarah Caulfield
Diatribe from the Library - Farrell Greenwald Brenner
Blind Girl Grunt - Constance Merritt
Acid and Tender - Jen Rouse
Beautiful Machinery - Wendy DeGroat
Odd Mercy - Gail Thomas
The Great Scissor Hunt - Jessica K. Hylton
A Bracelet of Honeybees - Lynn Strongin
Whirlwind @ Lesbos - Risa Denenberg
The Body's Alphabet - Ann Tweedy
First name Barbie last name Doll - Maureen Bocka
Heaven to Me - Abe Louise Young
Sticky - Carter Steinmann
Tiger Laughs When You Push - Ruth Lehrer
Night Ringing - Laura Foley
Paper Cranes - Dinah Dietrich
On Loving a Saudi Girl - Carina Yun
The Burn Poems - Lynn Strongin
I Carry My Mother - Lesléa Newman
Distant Music - Joan Annsfire
The Awful Suicidal Swans - Flower Conroy
Joy Street - Laura Foley
Chiaroscuro Kisses - G.L. Morrison
The Lillian Trilogy - Mary Meriam
Lady of the Moon - Amy Lowell, Lillian Faderman, Mary Meriam
Irresistible Sonnets - ed. Mary Meriam
Lavender Review - ed. Mary Meriam

www.ingramcontent.com/pod-product-compliance
Lightning Source LLC
Chambersburg PA
CBHW070050070426
42449CB00012BA/3217